St Antholin's Lectureship
Charity Lecture 2017

And The Light Shineth In Darkness

Faith, Reason and Knowledge in the Reformation

Kirsten Birkett

And The Light Shineth In Darkness: Faith, Reason and Knowledge in the Reformation)© Kirsten Birkett 2017

ISBN 978-1-906327-48-4

Cover photo: Illuminated cobbled street in old city by night © pyty – fotolia.com.

Published by the Latimer Trust May 2017

The Latimer Trust (formerly Latimer House, Oxford) is a conservative Evangelical research organisation within the Church of England, whose main aim is to promote the history and theology of Anglicanism as understood by those in the Reformed tradition. Interested readers are welcome to consult its website for further details of its many activities.

The Latimer Trust
c/o Oak Hill College
London N14 4PS UK
Registered Charity: 1084337
Company Number: 4104465
Web: www.latimertrust.org
E-mail: administrator@latimertrust.org

Views expressed in works published by The Latimer Trust are those of the authors and do not necessarily represent the official position of The Latimer Trust.

CONTENTS

1. Introduction 1
    - 1.1. *Knowledge: some historical background* 2
    - 1.2. *Aquinas* 3
2. Luther 7
3. Calvin 19
    - 3.1. *Augustine* 19
    - 3.2. *John Calvin* 22
4. Conclusion 34
    - 4.1. *Further reading:* 34

St. Antholin's Lectureship Charity Lectures 35

1. Introduction

The Bible describes a fallen world and fallen humanity, in which minds are darkened. We reject God, and suppress the truth about him. How, then, can we know him at all? In other words, what are the noetic effects of sin? During the Reformation, doctrines of total depravity and the effects of the fall on the whole person re-emerged, with consequent implications for epistemology. If minds are fallen, how can we expect to know anything accurately? The purpose of this study is to start to answer that question by looking at some of the epistemology we find emerging from the writings of John Calvin and Martin Luther.

Of course epistemology never stands on its own. The classical view that epistemology, ontology and ethics influence and rest upon each other is borne out in the history of ideas. The nature of what exists (ontology) affects what we can know about it (epistemology) and therefore what we should do about it (ethics). Expanding this idea further, we could point out that ontology includes anthropology, our own nature as humans. We are the knowers we are concerned with.

For this reason, we are not just interested in what Calvin and Luther said explicitly about knowledge. After all, knowledge and epistemology *per se* were not topics they were most concerned with – they were theologians and apologists, not philosophers (although Calvin's systematising brought his ideas more conveniently into accessible categories). However both Luther and Calvin did write quite a lot about the fall and its effects on the whole person; what our reason can do and accomplish, and how it relates to faith pre- and post- fall; what it means that we are created for and by God; as well as who God is himself. All of these issues affect us as knowers.

This is not at all a comprehensive study in Reformation epistemology; that would be a different work. This is more an investigation into certain themes about the mind and knowing, and how we should think about such things given Reformation theology.

1.1. Knowledge: some historical background

Knowledge has always been a problem as long as there has been Western philosophy, but arguably not since there has been theology. The Old Testament answer to the question of how we know God is clear: God speaks. We hear and therefore know, because he is the God of truth (Is 65:16) and he is perfect in knowledge (Job 37:16). 'You are God, and your words are true,' David says to God in 2 Sam 7:28. Knowledge – of anything – begins with God (Prov 1:7); and the corollary of this is that any thinking that does not start with the knowledge of God are not worth having (Col 2:8). If there is a problem of knowledge, it lies with us, not with God or the possibility of knowledge.

In Greek thought it was not nearly so clear. For the two most famous thinkers, if anything, it was the other way around. The assumption we find in both Plato and Aristotle is that we are capable of knowing, but need to find the right way to do it. Just what that right way was, however, proved elusive. Plato, in the end, was unable to provide a satisfactory account for knowledge, although it was a key concern of his. Aristotle, who recognised Plato's problems, did not ultimately solve them. Both had a high view of human capacity to have knowledge of reality – although their definitions of just what this was differed – but both found it difficult to pin down. The response of the Sceptics was to find the whole quest just too bothersome, and to give up in the interests of an easy life.[1]

Where Plato fundamentally disagrees with Aristotle over knowledge is that Plato rejects the senses as a source of knowledge. The senses, he holds, can always be deceived; they are fallible, and the world they perceive is always changing. In the end, the only things

---

[1] See Plato, *Theatetus* (trans. Robin Waterfield; London: Penguin, 1987), *Meno* (trans. W. K. C. Guthrie; Harmondsworth: Penguin, 1956) and *Republic* (trans. Desmond Lee; London: Penguin, 1955); Aristotle *Metaphysics* (trans. W. D. Ross; London: Penguin, 2004); for the Sceptics, Sextus Empiricus *Outlines of Scepticism* (trans. Jonathan Barnes; Cambridge, Cambridge University Press, 2000).

that can be known, the only things to which 'knowledge' could possible refer, are the eternal forms.[2]

Of course, this is a problem if you don't believe in eternal forms. Aristotle did not, and so brought knowledge into this changeable world of sense-data. The Sceptics responded to this faith in the ability of the human intellect to find knowledge with pessimism. It is easy, as we have seen in the subsequent history of ideas, to do either. Both faith in human rationality, and scepticism about it, however, require justification. What Christianity and Christian thinkers would do is ground human knowledge theologically. As we move into the Middle Ages, we find that although many of the ideas of both Plato and Aristotle were absorbed and deliberately harmonised, the premises had moved godwards.

1.2. Aquinas

It is often said in summary that Aquinas did not believe the intellect was fallen. This is a generalisation which (as if often the case with Aquinas) needs qualification. Aquinas held that the natural virtues were still available – prudence, justice, temperance and courage – even though the supernatural ones – faith, hope and love – were no longer achievable.

Aquinas did certainly think the intellect was in one sense wounded in the fall.

> Through the gift of original justice the spiritual part in man had perfect hold over the inferior powers of soul, while it itself was perfected by God as being subject to him. As has been said, original justice was taken away by the sin of the first parents. As a result all the powers of the soul are in a sense lacking the order proper to them, their natural order to virtue, and the deprivation is called the 'wounding of nature'. Now there are four powers of soul which are apt subjects of virtue: reason, in which there is prudence; will, where justice is; the irascible appetite, in which

---

[2] See Plato, *Republic*, Book V (Lee: 196-204), VI (Lee: 237-240) and VII (Lee 241-248).

there is courage; the concupiscible appetite, where temperance is. In so far as reason is deprived of its direction towards truth, we have the 'wound of ignorance'.[3]

To what extent did this wounding diminish the soul's power of reason? As this quotation says, reason is no longer directed towards virtue; but 'the principles constitutive of nature together with the properties derived from them, for example the powers of soul and the like' are 'neither destroyed nor lessened through sin'.[4] That is, it would seem that while the intellect is wounded in its direction, it is still functional.

We are still, through our natural powers, able to know God. In Aquinas' thinking, God's existence is not a self-evident truth, or at least not to us. Aquinas thought that there was only a vague innate knowledge of God: 'the awareness that God exists is not implanted in us by nature in any clear or specific way'.[5] However we know, and can know, God through his effects: 'God's effects...can serve to demonstrate that God exists, even though they cannot help us to know him comprehensively for what he is.'[6] Aquinas expands upon this when he writes on knowledge. Although we cannot in the present life understand immaterial substances, we can know material ones.

> Thus we must say simply that God is not the first thing known by us. Rather we arrive at a knowledge of God by way of creatures, as St Paul says, The invisible things of God are there for the mind to see in the things he has made. Instead, what is understood first by us in the present life is the whatness of material things, which is the object of our intellect, as said many times before.[7]

Because this knowledge starts from material things, it means that we begin to know God through our senses. This is, in fact, how we know

---

[3] Thomas Aquinas, *Summa Theologiae* (Gen. ed. Thomas Gilby; 60 vols; London and New York: Eyre &Spottiswoode and McGraw-Hill, 1964) I.ii.Q85.A3 (ST 26:91).
[4] Aquinas, *Summa* I.ii.Q85.A1 (ST26:81).
[5] Aquinas, *Summa* I.Q2.A1 (ST 2:7).
[6] Aquinas, *Summa* I.Q2.A1 (ST2:11).
[7] Aquinas, *Summa* 1.Q88.A3 (ST 12:135).

anything: beginning from material things,[8] then abstracting and reasoning from them. This does not give us certain specific knowledge of God, for example that he is trinity; revelation is needed for that. But certainly what can be demonstrated from creation is significant. This upholds a very positive view of fallen intellectual capacities, for it is held that any thinker capable of following the logic can see the truth of these propositions (although it is all right simply to accept them by faith, since the logic still holds). This is natural, inferential knowledge of God.

> The truths about God which St Paul says we can know by our natural powers of reasoning – that God exists, for example – are not numbered among the articles of faith, but are presupposed to them. For faith presupposes natural knowledge, just as grace does nature and all perfections that which they perfect. However, there is nothing to stop a man accepting on faith some truth which he personally cannot demonstrate, even if that truth in itself is such that demonstration could make it evident.[9]

Aquinas' emphasis on natural theology follows from this. Our minds have the power to organise sense data and demonstrate truth through deductive reasoning. This is why our minds can prove the existence of God, as Aquinas does in his five ways.[10]

Revelation, then, supplements and completes what can be known through natural reason.

> We also stood in need of being instructed by divine revelation even in religious matters the human reason is able to investigate. For the rational truth about God would have appeared only to few, and even so after a long time and mixed with many mistakes; whereas on knowing this depends our whole welfare, which is in God.[11]

---

[8] Aquinas, *Summa* 1.Q84.A8 (ST 12:45).
[9] Aquinas, *Summa* 1.Q2.A2 (ST 2:11).
[10] Aquinas, *Summa* 1.Q2.A3 (ST 2:13).
[11] Aquinas, *Summa* 1.Q1.A1 (ST 1:7).

Human reason, at least in those with some ability, is able to investigate created things, and indeed many religious matters; revelation perfects human knowledge. There is no sense in which Aquinas is against Scripture. Christian theology, the 'divine science', is about 'truth which comes through revelation, not through natural reasoning'.[12] Nevertheless, natural reasoning can still accomplish quite a lot, even in knowledge of God.

---

[12] Aquinas, *Summa* I.Q1.A6 (ST 1:23).

2. Luther

What a difference, then, when we come to Martin Luther, who tells us 'the intellect has become darkened, so that we no longer know God and his will and no longer perceive the works of God'.[1]

Luther has for a long time been known as an irrationalist, opposed to reason and with a rather boorish contempt for philosophy and rationality in religion. This on its own I have always found hard to square with the fact that Luther was a highly educated and highly intelligent scholar. As one of my PhD supervisors pointed out, Luther understood medieval theology far better than I ever will.

Luther, nonetheless, was always a contentious writer and speaker, and did not write any work on epistemology or philosophy *per se*. His writings were mostly polemical and in the interests of salvation for sinners. His opinions on epistemology are expressed in texts scattered throughout his corpus. However they are there, and they reveal that while Luther had a healthy appreciation of the fallenness of humanity, including the fallenness of the mind, he was no irrationalist.

Luther accepted the possibility of knowledge, in many areas. We can have, for instance, historical knowledge; he wrote of Genesis teaching 'historical facts', emphasising that this is how the book should be read, not as allegory.[2] Luther was also positive towards the natural sciences. He contrasted sciences that can be known with, for instance, astrology which is to be rejected because it cannot be demonstrated.

> So far as this matter is concerned, however, I shall never be convinced that astrology should be numbered among the sciences. And I shall adhere to this opinion because astrology is

---

[1] Martin Luther, 'Lectures on Genesis' in *Luther's Works* (eds Jaroslav Pelikan and Helmut T. Lehmann; 55 vols; St Louis and Philadelphia: Concordia and Fortress Press) (LW 1:114).
[2] Luther, 'Lectures on Genesis' (LW 1:93).

entirely without proof. The appeal to experience has no effect on me. All the astrological experiences are purely individual cases. The experts have taken note of and recorded only those instances which did not fail; but they took no note of the rest of the attempts, where they were wrong and the results which they predicted as certain did not follow. Aristotle says that one swallow does not make a spring, and so I do not believe that from such partial observations a science can be established.[3]

This is a sensible empirical principle, to evaluate all observations, not just ones that prove your theory. The point is that astrology does not, therefore, rest on observations; knowledge of the stars is possible, but astrology does not demonstrate that it is the discipline that possesses it.

For a man so positive in many ways about knowledge and our capacity to gain it, Luther nonetheless wrote frequently in a disparaging way against reason, and he could be very damning. His strong language makes for memorable quotations – 'reason is the devil's whore' certainly sticks in the mind. However in his loquaciousness he is also very ready to explain exactly what he means, and is entirely clear. For instance, this extract from *Table Talk*:

> [The question was asked,] Is the light of reason also useful [to theology]? [Martin Luther answered:] I make a distinction. Reason that is under the devil's control is harmful, and the more clever and successful it is, the more harm it does. We see this in the case of learned men who on the basis of their reason disagree with the Word. On the other hand, when illuminated by the Holy Spirit, reason helps to interpret the Holy Spirit. So Cochlaeus' tongue speaks blasphemies while my tongue speaks God's praise. Nevertheless, it is the same instrument in both of us. It is a tongue, whether before or after faith. The tongue, as a tongue, doesn't contribute to faith, and yet it serves faith when the heart is illuminated. So reason, when illuminated, helps faith by

---

[3] Luther, 'Lectures on Genesis' (LW 1:44).

> reflecting on something, but reason without faith isn't and can't be helpful. Without faith the tongue utters nothing but blasphemies ... But reason that's illuminated takes all its thoughts from the Word. The substance remains and the unreal disappears when reason is illuminated by the Spirit.[4]

As Luther makes clear, reason is an instrument that can be used for good or bad. Without faith, reason does not have the right information to work on, so will come to wrong conclusions.

Also, reason can have false criteria for judgement. Being sinful, it tends to underestimate the seriousness and power of sin, and also the glory of God's character. For instance:

> Our Lord God is always in the wrong, no matter what he does. He condemned Adam for disobedience when he ate of the fruit of the tree. Reason considers only the object of obedience, and so God is said to have gone too far. On the other hand, God freely forgives all sins, even the crucifixion of his Son, provided men believe, and this is also regarded as going too far. Who can bring these two into harmony – the greatest severity and the greatest liberty and indulgence (as it seems to reason)? Therefore it is said, 'Become like children'.[5]

Reason is contrasted to faith here, because to our (fallen) reason God's judgement and mercy are both unreasonable. It is not that reason as a faculty is the enemy of faith, but when used with wrong assumptions, it will misjudge truth.

However, for believers, reason is an 'excellent instrument'. It becomes useful, when working properly. 'Faith is now furthered by reason, speech and eloquence, whereas these were only impediments prior to faith. Enlightened reason, taken captive by faith, receives life from faith, for it is slain and given life again.' In believers, reason 'doesn't fight against faith but promotes it' – just as speech now

---

4   Luther, 'Table Talk' (LW 54:71).
5   Luther, 'Table Talk' (LW 54:105).

praises God, doing something useful whereas before conversion it did not.

Luther shows a very instrumental opinion of reason in these comments. 'David used a bow, a sword, and weapons and he said, 'Not in bow do I trust', but he didn't spurn the weapons.' The vain use of reason is discarded, not reason itself. 'Reason, speech, and all gifts and created things are therefore different in believers and Christians than in unbelievers.'[6]

Far from rejecting reason, then, Luther insists that faith makes reason reasonable rather than vain. Reason is a good tool, it just needs to be used properly; something that can't happen without faith. Nonetheless, there are things which are not discovered even by enlightened reason without revelation. 'Articles of faith, like the Trinity and the incarnation of Christ – these don't tally with reason'. This is not to say that such things are irrational; but they may be beyond our capacity to understand. People can also have different levels of spiritual understanding. 'Paul understood a good part of it, though he didn't comprehend all of it by any means.'[7]

For this reason, study of Scripture requires humility on the part of the believer. Those with too much trust in their own ability will not understand it as well as the humble Christian who asks God for help. 'The Holy Scriptures require a humble reader who shows reverence and fear toward the Word of God and constantly says, 'Teach me, teach me, teach me!' The Spirit resists the proud.'[8]

Why is it, then, that Luther is best known for his disparagement of reason? He certainly provides fodder for those determined to prove him an irrationalist. 'Reason is the devil's whore' is a key example. However for all that this is quoted with glee on atheist or humanist websites, finding anyone who knows where he said it, much less has read the original context, is far more rare. Luther actually compared

---

[6] Luther, 'Table Talk' (LW 54:183-4).
[7] Luther, 'Table Talk' (LW 43:377-8).
[8] Luther, 'Table Talk' (LW 54:378).

reason to a whore more than once, but again, it is in the context of the wrong use of reason. In his last sermon in Wittenberg, for instance, he was writing of the continued need for Scripture given that even though we are saved, we remain sinners. The 'old man and his works' – the sinful nature – continually try to lead us astray, even using reason to justify wrong ideas and doctrine; for human reason, under sinful impulses, will claim 'that everything that pops into its head and the devil puts into its heart is the Holy Spirit'.[9] What Scripture calls idolatry, fallen reason calls wisdom and holiness. Here Luther is not against rationality, so much as rationalising; using one's gift of reason to justify sin, rather than to resist it.

> The prophets say: You must not serve God on the mountains or in the valleys or under the trees, but in Jerusalem, which is the place that God appointed for his worship and where his word is. But here again, reason says: True enough, I have been called, circumcised, and adjured to go to Jerusalem, but here is a beautiful meadow, a fine green mountain; if we worship God here this will please God and all the angels in heaven. After all, is God the kind of God who binds himself only to Jerusalem? Such wisdom of reason the prophets call whoredom.[10]

Such 'reason', using semi-biblical premises and ignoring other information from Scripture, is only too common today. It was the same in Luther's time: reason without the Word to guide it will be used for sinful purposes. It will create wrong theology and come to wrong conclusions about God. Luther's conclusion, however, is never to reject reason: it is to emphasise the need for the Word, and good teachers of it.

Luther is also famous for denigrating the study of philosophy, saying that one should only study it in order to destroy it. This

---

[9] Luther, 'Last sermon at Wittenberg' (LW 51:373-4).
[10] Luther, 'Last sermon at Wittenberg' (LW 51:374). Luther similarly calls reason the devil's prostitute in *Against the Heavenly Prophets in the Matter of Images and Sacraments* (LW40:175). In this very angry piece, Luther again is not criticising reason as such but poor reasoning from Scripture.

statement occurs in his lectures on Romans, which he presented in 1515 – very early in his career, before the 95 theses. Here his concern is eschatological. Given that creation is waiting for an end to its frustration (Rom 8:19), the focus being the end times, how foolish to devote so much effort simply to considering creation as it now is.

> As a result the foolishness of the philosopher is like a man who, joining himself to a builder and marvelling at the cutting and hewing and measuring of the wood and the beams, is foolishly content and quiet among these things, without concern as to what the builder finally intends to make by all of these exertions.[11]

Given Luther's famous passion for the gospel – which drove the Reformation and dominated his life – these remarks are not surprising, as he urges students to spend their lives in what really matters, not in studies concerning vain things; like the apostle, who 'calls our attention away from a consideration of the present and from the essence and accidents of things and directs us to their future state'.[12]

For the purposes of the current study, we, however, are still interested in at least one aspect of the present – what we, fallen creatures, can know – and to that end we now consider that Luther also looked to the past, in this respect. Part of what we glean about Luther's views on knowledge come from the considerable interest he showed in the condition of the pre-fallen Adam. In his lectures on Genesis, Luther devoted a fair amount of space to Adam's intellect and his knowledge of God, and how that changed in the fall.

Luther saw Adam as having a far greater intellectual capacity pre-fall, and therefore not just more knowledge than we have now, but much more direct access to knowledge.

> In Adam there was an enlightened reason, a true knowledge of God, and a most sincere desire to love God and his neighbour, so that Adam embraced Eve and at once acknowledged her to be his

---

[11] Luther, 'Lectures on Romans' (LW 25:361-2).
[12] Luther, 'Lectures on Romans' (LW 25:360).

own flesh. Added to these were other lesser but exceedingly important gifts – if you draw a comparison with our weakness – namely, a perfect knowledge of the nature of the animals, the herbs, the fruits, the trees, and the remaining creatures.[13]

Adam, not rebellious or fallen as we are, therefore knew God and loved him rightly – two things which Luther sees as inseparable. These things were natural for Adam. Also, as part of his power of dominion, he had a much enhanced knowledge of creation. He was able to know the animals simply by looking at them, and thus was able to name them. He knew of the stars and all of astronomy. Eve too 'had these mental gifts in the same degree as Adam'; not just knowledge of beasts, but 'her very nature was pure and full of the knowledge of God to such a degree that by herself she knew the Word of God and understood it'.[14]

We, however, after the fall, still have dominion but in a very reduced and feeble way. 'What we achieve in life, however, is brought about, not by the dominion which Adam had but through industry and skill. Thus we see the birds and the fish caught by cunning and deceit; and by skill the beasts are tamed...'.[15] We have not just lost knowledge, but a 'fullness of joy and bliss which Adam derived from his contemplation of all the animal creatures'. Our faculties, in contrast are 'leprous, dull and utterly dead'.[16] Moreover, and far worse, we no longer have Adam's immediate knowledge of God, which comes through perfect love of God.

Incidentally, we get here some tantalising comments from Luther about the nature of knowledge of creation, and how that has changed post-fall. In criticising Aristotle and other philosophers who have wrong views about creation, Luther recommends instead turning to Scripture. It is not that Scripture will necessarily give us better details about created things; indeed, he writes of the secular books 'with

---

[13] Luther, 'Lectures on Genesis' (LW 1:63).
[14] Luther, 'Lectures on Genesis' (LW 1:66-67).
[15] Luther, 'Lectures on Genesis' (LW 1:67).
[16] Luther, 'Lectures on Genesis' (LW 1:66).

descriptions of the natures of plants and animals' not to disparage them, but simply to point out how laborious a task it now is to gather such information, in contrast to Adam's immediate apprehension.[17] Rather, he recommends looking to Scripture because precisely what we lack in knowledge from simply observing the world, is where it came from and what it is for.

> Therefore let us learn that true wisdom is in Holy Scripture and in the Word of God. This gives information not only about the matter of the entire creation, not only about its form, but also about the efficient and final cause, about the beginning and about the end of all things, about who did the creating and for what purpose he created. Without the knowledge of these two causes our wisdom does not differ much from that of the beasts, which also make use of their eyes and ears but are utterly without knowledge about their beginning and their end.[18]

Here we have what we might consider an endorsement of empirical science, in anything but its modern triumphal context. We can indeed have a certain wisdom about creation from our eyes and ears – but without the right framework, without knowing the creator who made it or its purpose in being made, what do we really know? It is knowledge, but minimal. It is not what really matters about creation.

Luther spelled this out more concisely in the *Disputation Concerning Man* (1536), where he asserted 'it is certainly true that reason is the most important and the highest in rank among all things and, in comparison with other things of this life, the best and something divine; it is the inventor and mentor of all the arts, medicines, laws, and of whatever wisdom, power, virtue, and glory men possess in this life.'[19] However, the problem with this ability is that 'in spite of the fact that it is of such majesty, it does not know itself *a priori*, but only *a posteriori*' – reason only knows 'after the fact', on the basis of evidence, it does not know itself. 'Therefore', he goes

---

[17] Luther, 'Lectures on Genesis' (LW 1:120).
[18] Luther, 'Lectures on Genesis' (LW 1:125).
[19] Luther, 'Disputation Concerning Man' (LW 34:137).

on, 'if philosophy or reason itself is compared with theology, it will appear that we know almost nothing about man.' How is that?

> Inasmuch as we seem scarcely to perceive his material cause sufficiently. For philosophy does not know the efficient cause for certain, nor likewise the final cause, because it posits no other final cause than the peace of this life, and does not know that the efficient cause is God the creator.[20]

Even our material cause – what we are made of, how we work and so on – we scarcely perceive sufficiently. What we are here for, who made us and why; those things are completely beyond our natural powers.

Indeed, in commenting on Psalm 51 Luther wrote:

> We cannot say that the natural powers are perfect even in civil matters. We see what great contempt there is for laws that prescribe what is right, how great is the breakdown of the discipline on account of which God instituted laws and authority. A physician is often deceived in mixing drugs, and sometimes by his inexperience he kills a sick man. Thus the very light of the eyes, the ears, and all the other organs acquired a fault through sin. They are not as sound and perfect as they were in Adam before sin. This corruption of the senses is obvious. Now what condition do you suppose exists in spiritual matters?[21]

So in the fall, much of the excellence of intellect and knowledge that Adam and Eve possessed was lost. Far worse, however, was the fall of the will. Before Adam's fall, 'his will was good and sound; moreover, his reason or intellect was sound, so that whatever God wanted or said, man also wanted, believed, and understood the same thing.'[22] Afterwards, although the loss of enlightened reason is bad,

> [t]he most serious loss consists in this, that not only were those

---

[20] Luther, 'Disputation concerning man' (LW 34:137-138).
[21] Luther, 'Psalm 51' (LW 12:309).
[22] Luther, 'Lectures on Genesis' (LW 1:141).

benefits lost, but man's will turned away from God. As a result, man wants and does none of the things God wants and commands. Likewise, we have no knowledge about what God is, what grace is, what righteousness is, and finally what sin itself is.[23]

It is the perfect harmony with God and his wishes that is the most tragic loss. *That* knowledge is what really matters, and which we no longer have. Therefore, while our reason now might work well enough for mundane matters, it is inherently crippled. Aristotle said 'reason pleads for the best' (reason tells what is best to do); but:

I do not deny that these statements are true when they are applied to matters that are subject to reason: to managing cattle, building a house, and sowing a field. But in higher matters they are not true. How can a reason which hates God be called sound? How can a will which resists God's will and refuses to obey God be called good? Therefore when they say: 'Reason pleads for the best', you should say, 'For the best in a mundane sense, that is, in things about which reason can judge'... Therefore in theology let us maintain that reason in men is most hostile to God, and that the respectable will is most opposed to the will of God.[24]

Indeed, after the fall, Adam and Eve show a distinct lack of reason:

...is it not the height of stupidity, in the first place, to attempt the impossible, to try to avoid God, whom they cannot avoid? In the second place, to attempt to avoid Him is so stupid a way, that they believe themselves safe among the trees, when iron walls and huge masses of mountains could not save them?[25]

It would seem, then, as though reason after the fall is fairly useless; only fit for use in the most mundane things. The comparison with the pre-fall Adam and Eve, however, should not be taken this way. Although Luther held that we are far inferior to our pre-fall ancestors,

---

[23] Luther, 'Lectures on Genesis' (LW 1:141).
[24] Luther, 'Lectures on Genesis' (LW 1:143).
[25] Luther, 'Lectures on Genesis' (LW 1:172).

nonetheless he still wrote at times with a fairly high view of human capacity, even if very qualified by the reality of sin.

There is, nonetheless, a final way in which Luther cast aspersions on reason, and this is in the human tendency to what he calls 'inquisitiveness'. It is wonderful that God has given us so much knowledge of himself, and we should rejoice in that; but there is also a danger in seeking to know too much about God. 'Why not rather let God keep his decisions and mysteries in secret? We have no reason to exert ourselves so much that these decisions and mysteries be revealed to us.'[26] We should beware trying to investigate 'above or outside the revelation of God' – such things are simply none of our concern. Perhaps wary of church traditions that insisted on knowledge of God outside of Scripture, Luther very firmly preached strict limits to theological inquiry. Such inquisitiveness is original sin itself, wanting to find a way to God 'through natural speculation' – which is not just sinful but futile, since the only way to the Father is through Christ.

> Furthermore, God has most sternly forbidden this investigation of the divinity. Thus when the apostles ask in Acts 1:6, "Has it not been predestined that at this time the kingdom should be restored?" Christ says to them: "It is not for you to know the times". "Let me be hidden where I have not revealed myself to you", says God, "or you will be the cause of your own destruction, just as Adam fell in a horrible manner; for he who investigates my majesty will be overwhelmed by my glory".[27]

The moral is: knowledge is possible. Reason is a valuable gift, and we should use it. But both should be put firmly within the context of God's revelation. As fallen creatures, we have lost our immediate knowledge of God and his will, as well as of the rest of creation. Now, we are able and should use reason to know the world, but it will be laborious and hard work. When it comes to the things of God, only Scripture can provide the context for reason to work properly.

---

[26] Luther, 'Lectures on Genesis' (LW 5:44).
[27] Luther, 'Lectures on Genesis' (LW 5:44).

Scripture must be the starting point for reason – it provides our premises and the information we cannot and will never have outside it. Scripture also sets the boundaries of what we should seek to know, especially about God. We must therefore approach Scripture humbly, ready to listen and slow to question.

> With regard to this I always say that faith must have absolutely nothing but the Word on its side and must permit no subtle argumentation or human ideas in addition. Otherwise it is impossible for faith to be retained and preserved. For human wisdom and reason cannot progress beyond judging and concluding in accordance with what it sees and feels or with what it comprehends with the senses But faith must transcend such feeling and understanding or make its decision contrary to these and cling to whatever the Word submits. Reason and human competence do not enable faith to do that, but this is the work of the Holy Spirit on the heart of man.[28]

For Luther, it is God's word that gives us knowledge, and therefore a place for reason; but reason must not be set up against it. In the Word we can have absolute confidence precisely because it is from God. If reason doubts the word of God, this is reason being foolish and denying true wisdom. The wisdom that looks to God in humble obedience, however, will find truth.

> This sort of doctrine, which reveals the Son of God, is not taught, learned, or judged by any human wisdom or by the Law itself; it is revealed by God, first by the external Word and then inwardly through the Spirit. Therefore the Gospel is a divine Word that came down from heaven and is revealed by the Holy Spirit, who was sent for this very purpose.[29]

---

[28] Luther, 'Sermon on 1 Corinthians 15' (LW 28:68-69).
[29] Luther, 'Lectures on Galatians' (LW 26:73).

3. Calvin

In many ways, Calvin's theology brought Augustine back to the fore. While Luther certainly knew and quoted Augustine's works, for Calvin in particular Augustine is important background. So in entirely unchronological order, we will take the opportunity here to review some of Augustine's thoughts on epistemology.

3.1. Augustine

Augustine was writing in the context of late antiquity. He moved in his own life from a commitment to neoPlatonism, through other views, to Christianity. One of his first projects as a Christian was to attack the views of the ancient Sceptics.

Augustine refuted scepticism and the view that any knowledge statement might be wrong, by demonstrating that there are some statements he knew to be right. For the Academics, one of the Ancient schools of scepticism, the way to wisdom was by never allowing oneself to consent to error. Since any statement could possibly be wrong, nothing can be known, and so one must then never consent to any knowledge claim. This, they held, was wisdom. Yet Augustine said that people who admit they know nothing of the truth can hardly be called wise. Truth is indeed knowable.

> Even I, however, who am still far from being anyway near being a wise man, know something at any rate in physics. I am certain, for instance, that there is one world or not one. If there is not one world, then the number of worlds is finite or infinite...Likewise, I know that this world of ours is ordered as it is, either the intrinsic nature of corporeal matter, or by some providence; that it either always was and always will be, or began to be and will never cease, or never exist forever. I know countless things about physics after this manner. These disjunctions are true, and no one can refute them by pointing to any likeness in them to what

is not true.[1]

Augustine, then, held that knowledge is possible. We can know it because God – 'the intelligible Light, in, by and through whom and through whom all intelligible things are illumined' – illuminates our minds.[2]

> The mind has, as it were, eyes of its own, analogous to the soul's senses. The certain truths of the sciences are analogous to the objects which the sun's rays make visible, such as the earth and earthly things. And it is God himself who illumines all.[3]

More than that, he held that we are capable of grasping eternal truths, which are grounded in God. How can we grasp such things? Because we are illuminated by God. Even knowledge of things in the world is not possible without God's illumination; even more so, it is necessary for knowledge of God. Our knowledge of God's existence, like our knowledge of our own existence, is immediate and intuitive. Knowledge, then, is not primarily from sense experience, but begins with this awareness. Illumination by God is the only way knowledge of him is possible.

This differs from Aquinas' view that the preambles to articles of faith could be known by natural reason; for Augustine, faith had to come first. This gave rise to his famous dictum which can be summarised as 'faith seeking understanding'.

> If you have not understood, I say, believe. For understanding is the recompense of faith. Therefore, seek not to understand so that you may believe, but believe so that you may understand.[4]

---

[1] Augustine, *Against the Academics* (trans. John J. O'Meara; New York: Newman Press, 1951) 3.10.23;125. See also *On the Trinity* (ed. Philip Schaff; *Nicene and Post-Nicene Fathers*, vol III; Edinburgh: T&T Clark, 1998) XV.12 (Schaff 211).

[2] Augustine, *Soliloquies*, (trans. John H. S. Burleigh; Philadelphia: The Westminster Press, 1980) 1.3., 24.

[3] Augustine, *Soliloquies* 1.12 (Burleigh 30).

[4] Augustine, *Tractates on the Gospel of John 28-54*, Tractate 29.6 (trans. John W. Rettig, *The Fathers of the Church: A New Translation*, vol 88, Washington, DC: Catholic University of America Press, 1993) 18.

For Augustine, then, faith in God is the starting point, and so God's revelation is necessary. Reason on any other basis will not reach its ends. Once faith is in place, however, God's illumination allows reason to come to understanding of truth. Our capacity for truth rests not in the natural powers of our reason, but in God; it is rational, then, to begin with acknowledging dependence upon God.

When faith seeks understanding, the believer is seeking to comprehend and come to apprehend fully what has already been believed from the testimony of Scripture. Scripture is the source of the information for understanding; and the faith that trusts it as God's word is the vehicle for the illumination that makes reason profitable. We believe on the basis of the testimony, which is trustworthy because it is from God and has his authority. We will be in a position, then, to know fully what cannot be known without that revelation and without supernatural illumination. Augustine's complete dependence on God is evident throughout his writings.

This is not to denigrate reason; in fact, in some ways Augustine thinks of reason as being more important than faith. It is simply that faith is necessary before proper reason is possible. He starts from faith; once he is believing, he would then, by reasoning and thoughtful reading of Scripture, wish to understand what he believes in the fullest way possible. This can only happen when the mind is first cleansed – which happens through faith. He put this sentiment in the mouth of Reason itself:

> I, Reason, am in minds as the power of looking is in the eyes. Having eyes is not the same things as looking, and looking is not the same as seeing. The soul therefore needs three things: eyes which it can use aright, looking and seeing. The eye of the mind is healthy when it is pure from every taint of the body, that is, when it is remote and purged from desire of mortal things. And this, faith alone can give in the first place. It is impossible to show God to a mind vitiated and sick. Only the healthy mind can see him.[5]

---

[5] Augustine, *Soliloquies*, 1.12 (Burleigh 30).

Afterall, Augustine, who is often credited with first formulating the theology of original sin (we shall credit the Bible with first *teaching* it), held that we are entirely enslaved to sin. As he wrote in *City of God*:

> ... he who in his pride had pleased himself was by God's justice handed over to himself. But the result of this was not that he was in every way under his own control, but that he was at odds with himself, and lived a life of harsh and pitiable slavery, instead of the freedom he so ardently desired, a slavery under him with whom he entered into agreement in his sinning.[6]

Being slaves to sin, we cannot by our own power ever remove sin. Our wills are corrupt; we do not *want* to know God. Sin's effect on our whole person, including our minds, is not in our own power to heal. This background we keep in mind as we turn to Calvin's views on reason and knowledge.

3.2. *John Calvin*

Calvin begins the *Institutes* with knowledge; in particular, the knowledge of God and of ourselves.

> Nearly all the wisdom we possess, that is to say, true and sound wisdom, consists of two parts: the knowledge of God and of ourselves.[7]

This beginning also demonstrates that Calvin is not so interested in knowledge of other things. His attitude to knowledge in general, that is, knowledge of the external world, is important to him insofar as it reveals the creator, rather than being a topic he writes about for its own value. But knowledge of *ourselves* as a created thing leads to God; for Calvin, we cannot separate the experience of knowledge of God and knowledge of ourselves.

---

[6] Augustine, *Concerning the City of God Against the Pagans* (trans. Henry Bettenson; London: Penguin Books, 1972) XIV.15; 574-5.

[7] John Calvin, *Institutes of the Christian Religion* (ed. John T. McNeill; trans. Ford Lewis Battles; 2 vols; Philadephia: Westminster, 1980) I. i. i. (Battles 1:35).

> In the first place, no one can look upon himself without immediately turning his thoughts to the contemplation of God, in whom he "lives and moves".[8]

Why is this? Because our very sinfulness drives us to see God. 'The miserable ruin, into which the rebellion of the first man cast us, especially compels us to look upward'.[9] On the other hand, knowledge of God is necessary for true knowledge of ourselves. '[I]t is certain that man never achieves a clear knowledge of himself unless he has first looked upon God's face, and then descends from contemplating him to scrutinize himself'.[10]

This demonstrates what will become a theme throughout the *Institutes*: that knowledge is never neutral. What would become a truism of postmodern theology was present in this sixteenth-century writer, albeit in a theological form. However, even then, it was not a new idea; Calvin amply demonstrates what the ancients knew, that epistemology and ethics are never entirely separate; neither is ontology. It is precisely because of who God is, and who we are, that knowledge of God is not possible without piety. This is the topic for chapter II of the first book. 'Indeed, we shall not say that, properly speaking, God is known where there is no religion or piety'.[11] To know God properly, we must recognise him as sovereign God, the creator and the source of wisdom and truth. True knowledge of God is inseparable from a submissive response to God.

> For how can the thought of God penetrate your mind without your realizing immediately that, since you are his handiwork, you have been made over and bound to his command by right of creation?...Again, you cannot behold him clearly unless you acknowledge him to be the fountainhead and source of every good.[12]

---

[8] Calvin, *Institutes* I.i.1 (Battles 1: 35).
[9] Calvin, *Institutes* I.i.1 (Battles 1:36).
[10] Calvin, *Institutes* I.i.2 (Battles 1:37).
[11] Calvin, *Institutes* I.ii.1 (Battles 1:39).
[12] Calvin, *Institutes* I.ii.2 (Battles 1:42).

That would seem to be obvious: if we truly see God as God, as who he is, we must recognise our smallness before him. There is still an epistemological question, however. How do we start? How do we get to this knowledge? Calvin boldly reasserts an Augustinian doctrine in contrast to much medieval thought: this knowledge is innate and immediate.

> There is within the human mind, and indeed by natural instinct, an awareness of divinity. This we take to be beyond controversy.[13]

Such a claim would certainly not be beyond controversy now; however, as far as I am aware all we know of human ethnographic studies would seem to bear it out. All people, Calvin claims, have an innate knowledge of God. 'To prevent anyone from taking refuge in the pretense of ignorance, God himself has implanted in all men a certain understanding of his divine majesty.'[14] It is an immediate knowledge, by 'direct acquaintance' as Hoitenga puts it;[15] it is not through reasoning or proof, or belief acquired on testimony. God is directly present to people's understanding. Calvin also refers to this in his Commentary on John 1:5:

> The Evangelist anticipates this question, and first of all lays down this caution, that *the light* which was originally bestowed on men must not be estimated by their present condition; because in this corrupted and degenerate nature *light* has been turned into *darkness*. And yet he affirms that the light of understanding is not wholly extinguished; for, amidst the thick darkness of the human mind, some remaining sparks of the brightness still shine... But on the other hand, the Evangelist maintains that, in the midst of the *darkness*, there are still some remains of light, which show in some degree the divine power of Christ. The statement that that *the light shineth in darkness* is not at all intended for the commendation of depraved nature, but rather for taking away

---

[13] Calvin, *Institutes* I.iii.1 (Battles 1:43).
[14] Calvin, *Institutes* I.iii.1 (Battles 1:43).
[15] Dewey J. Hoitenga, Jr, *Faith and Reason from Plato to Plantinga: An Introduction to Reformed Epistemology* (Albany: State University of New York Press, 1991).

every excuse for ignorance...

> The *light* which still dwells in corrupt nature consists chiefly of two parts; for, first, all men naturally possess some seed of religion; and, secondly, the distinction between good and evil is engraven on their consciences.[16]

What is epistemologically interesting here is that this knowledge is something *immediately obvious* from creation. Calvin does not present an argument, along the lines of Aquinas' five ways; he simply asserts that this is obvious to all.

> We see that no long or toilsome proof is needed to elicit evidences that serve to illuminate and affirm the divine majesty; since from the few we have sampled at random, whithersoever you turn, it is clear that they are so very manifest and obvious that they can easily be observed with the eyes and pointed out with the finger.[17]

This is precisely why humanity is without an excuse. The knowledge of God as creator is clear, and there to be had. 'We must therefore admit in God's individual works – but especially in them as a whole – that God's powers are actually represented as in a painting. Thereby the whole of mankind is invited and attracted to recognition of him.'[18]

It is not just that God is knowable, but so is creation. Although Calvin does not say much about it, he clearly believes in the objective reality of creation, and that it is knowable, because it is God's creation. God sustains the universe and regulates it by his wisdom. The world is real and good, with a predictable structure.

> Lest anyone, then, be excluded from access to happiness, he not only sowed in men's minds that seed of religion of which we have spoken but revealed himself and daily discloses himself in the whole workmanship of the universe. As a consequence, men cannot open their eyes without being compelled to see him...But

---

[16] John Calvin, *Commentary on the Gospel According to John* (trans. William Pringle; Grand Rapids: Baker Book House, 1984) 33-34.
[17] Calvin, *Institutes* I.v.9 (Battles 1:61).
[18] Calvin, *Institutes* I.v.10 (Battles 1:63).

upon his individual works he has engraved unmistakable marks of this glory.[19]

Part of that structure, that God has built into his world, is precisely this natural awareness we have of God. This awareness stands in stark contrast to Aquinas' idea of a confused and unclear sense of God. Calvin thought all we could observe about the universe simply shouted God's presence.

> There are innumerable evidences both in heaven and on earth that declare his wonderful wisdom; not only those more recondite matters for the closer observation of which astronomy, medicine, and all natural science are intended, but also those which thrust themselves upon the sight of even the most untutored and ignorant persons, so that they cannot open their eyes without being compelled to witness them'.[20]

Sin does not destroy this awareness: 'Men of sound judgement will always be sure that a sense of divinity which can never be effaced is engraved upon men's minds'.[21] What is lost, however, is the right response to this knowledge. Sinners struggle against this conviction of God and try to cast it away with 'stupid hardness' in their minds. Despite the fact that the knowledge is immediate to everyone, sinners try their hardest to ignore it. '...it is not a doctrine that must first be learned in school, but one of which each of us is master from his mother's womb and which nature itself permits no one to forget, although many strive with every nerve to this end'.[22] God has sowed the seed of religion but it does not grow.[23] People even 'deliberately befuddle themselves' to the point where they can say there is no God: 'And it is God's just punishment of the wicked that fatness envelops their hearts, so that after they have closed their eyes, in seeing they

---

[19] Calvin, *Institutes* I.v.1 (Battles 1:51-52).
[20] Calvin, *Institutes* I.v.2 (Battles 1:53).
[21] Calvin, *Institutes* I.iii.3 (Battles 1:45).
[22] Calvin, *Institutes* I.iii.3 (Battles 1:46).
[23] Calvin, *Institutes* I.iv.1 (Battles 1:47).

see not'.[24] The knowledge is there, but not there; it makes humanity culpable precisely because it is both present, and dismissed.

The intellectual content, then, always comes with a moral and emotional response. For the unregenerate, that response will be rejection and disobedience, rebellion and hatred. Only those with the Spirit, with Christian faith, will have the right response. This qualifies Calvin's assertion of the knowledge of God, however; for without the right response there is no *true* knowledge.

How then can we ever have the right response that will ensure true knowledge? This is precisely why we need Scripture, as the heading of Book I, chapter vi I states: 'God bestows the actual knowledge of himself upon us only in the Scriptures'. Despite God's presence 'set forth' to us, 'it is needful that another and better help be added to direct us aright to the very Creator of the universe'.[25] And what is that better help? 'Scripture can communicate to us what the revelation in the creation cannot'.[26] The Spirit enlightens us; and to get the Spirit we need Scripture. 'From this we readily understand that we ought zealously to apply ourselves both to read and to hearken to Scripture if indeed we want to receive any gain and benefit from the Spirit of God'.[27] This emphasises Calvin's conviction that the Spirit and Scripture are not to be separated. Quoting 2 Cor 3:8, Calvin says 'the Holy Spirit so inheres in his truth, which he expresses in Scripture, that only when its proper reverence and dignity are given to the Word does the Holy Spirit show forth his power'.[28]

> The Word is the instrument by which the Lord dispenses the illumination of his Sprit to believers. For they know no other Spirit than him who dwelt and spoke in the apostles, and by whose oracles they are continually recalled to the hearing of the Word.[29]

---

[24] Calvin, *Institutes* I.iv.2 (Battles 1:48).
[25] Calvin, *Institutes* I.vi.1 (Battles 1:69).
[26] Calvin, *Institutes* heading to I.vi.4 (Battles 1:73).
[27] Calvin, *Institutes* I.ix.2 (Battles 1:94).
[28] Calvin, *Institutes* I.ix.3 (Battles 1:95).
[29] Calvin, *Institutes* I.ix.3 (Battles 1:96).

This gift of Scripture, illuminated by the Spirit, is absolutely necessary for is, for we are fallen. We had 'original nobility', bestowed upon Adam[30] but have been punished for our detestable crime.[31] The root of our sinfulness, the cause of the fall, was unfaithfulness, which led to ambition and pride with ungratefulness. The result was corruption.

> In place of wisdom, virtue, holiness, truth and justice, with which adornments he had been clad, there came forth the most filthy plagues, blindness, impotence, impurity, vanity, and injustice.[32]

Original sin is 'a hereditary depravity and corruption of our nature, diffused into all parts of the soul, which first makes us liable to God's wrath, then also brings forth in us those works which Scripture calls "works of the flesh" (Gal 5:19)'.[33]

All parts of the soul are affected.[34] Calvin describes the soul as having two faculties, understanding and will (or heart); and all parts of the person have fallen. 'For in his discussion of a corrupt nature Paul not only condemns the inordinate impulses of the appetites that are seen, but especially contends the mind is given over to blindness and the heart to depravity'.[35] Sin has a clear noetic effect, not to be downplayed. This is no slight damage; the mind is *blind*. Depravity rules the whole person.

> [F]or even though something of understanding and judgement remains as a residue along with the will, yet we shall not call a mind whole and sound that is both weak and plunged into deep darkness.[36]

It is not, however, as though we can no longer think at all. Reason could not be completely wiped out because it is a natural gift, 'by

---

[30] Calvin, *Institutes* II.i.3 (Battles 1:244).
[31] Calvin, *Institutes* II.i.4 (Battles 1:244).
[32] Calvin, *Institutes* II.i.5 (Battles 1:246).
[33] Calvin, *Institutes* II.i.8 (Battles 1:251).
[34] Calvin, *Institutes* II.I.9 (Battles 1:252).
[35] Calvin, *Institutes* II.i.9 (Battles 1:253).
[36] Calvin, *Institutes* II.ii.12 (Battles 1:270).

which man distinguishes between good and evil, and by which he understands and judges'. But now it is a 'misshapen ruin'. John 1:5, Calvin says, suggests that there are 'sparks' still left over. But the light is inefficient and ineffective.

> First, in man's perverted and degenerate nature some sparks still gleam. These show him to be a rational being, differing from brute beasts, because he is endowed with understanding. Yet, secondly, they show this light choked with dense ignorance, so that it cannot come forth effectively.[37]

But we should not go so far as to deny humanity's capacity to reason, especially about earthly matters. 'When we so condemn human understanding for its perpetual blindness as to leave it no perception of any object whatever, we not only go against God's Word, but also run counter to the experience of common sense'.[38] People still have curiosity and desire for truth, which shows we have some notion of what truth is; even if we fail to find truth and fall into vanity, and investigate 'empty and worthless things'.

Therefore, we can know some things. We are capable enough in 'things below', and even intelligent enough to 'taste something' of things above, although our reason tends to be careless when considering heavenly things.[39] Earthly things – government, household management, mechanical skills, the liberal arts – we are able to know these well enough. Man is a social animal so we are able to preserve society; we know fair dealing and order.[40] We are able to learn the liberal and manual arts – not through recollection as Plato said, but because we have natural ability. 'Therefore this evidence clearly testifies to a universal apprehension of reason and understanding by nature implanted in men'.[41] This degree of reason and understanding for earthly things is still a gift of God. When we

---

[37] Calvin, *Institutes* II.ii.12 (Battles 1:270).
[38] Calvin, *Institutes* II.ii.12 (Battles 1:271).
[39] Calvin, *Institutes* II.ii.13 (Battles 1:271-2).
[40] Calvin, *Institutes* II.ii.13 (Battles 1:272).
[41] Calvin, *Institutes* II.ii.14 (Battles 1:273).

see knowledge of such things in secular writers, 'let that admirable light of truth shining in them teach us that the mind of man, though fallen and perverted from its wholeness, is nevertheless clothed and ornamented with God's excellent gifts'.[42]

What is more, we should never despise any truth, because it is always the gift of the Spirit. The fact that such good things appear in the writings of pagans is no reason to reject it wholesale. It is still the good provision of God for our benefit. The Spirit of God is the sole fountain of truth; despising anything true, simply because it has a pagan source, is dishonouring to the Spirit.

> Shall we deny that the truth shone upon the ancient jurists who established civic order and discipline with such great equity? Shall we say that the philosophers were blind in their fine observation and artful description of nature? Shall we say that those men were devoid of understanding who conceived the art of disputation and taught us to speak reasonably? Shall we say that they are insane who developed medicine, devoting their labour to our benefit? What shall we say of all the mathematical sciences? Shall we consider them the ravings of madmen? No, we cannot read the writings of the ancients on these subjects without great admiration.[43]

These things are all from God, and are reason for gratitude on our part. In fact, even pagans recognised that 'the gods' were the inventors of these useful things.

This leaves Calvin with a careful balancing act in his view of natural knowledge. On the one hand, God has given gifts even to those who don't know him, enabling them to be 'sharp and penetrating in their investigation of inferior things'.[44] Even with human nature 'despoiled of its true good'[45] we are able to benefit from the physics, dialectic, mathematics and so on of the ungodly. On

---

[42] Calvin, *Institutes* II.ii.15 (Battles 1:273).
[43] Calvin, *Institutes* II.ii.15 (Battles 1:274).
[44] Calvin, *Institutes* II.ii.15 (Battles 1:274).
[45] Calvin, *Institutes* II.ii.15 (Battles 1:275).

the other hand, this ability is still nothing to boast about. It should not be rejected, but we should not consider anyone truly blessed simply because 'he is credited with possessing great power to comprehend truth under the elements of this world'.[46] It is by God's grace that we still have any reason at all. He could have destroyed our nature entirely. The fact that some are cleverer than others is itself proof that this is a gift of God, 'which, in passing many by, declares itself bound to none'.[47]

When it comes to spiritual things, however, the fallen human is very limited. In knowing God, and knowing his salvation, 'the greatest geniuses are blinder than moles!'[48] For all his respect of the ancients, Calvin is fairly scathing about their theological insight. The philosophers occasionally make competent statements about God, but always with a 'certain giddy imagination'.[49] God would occasionally give them truth to say, but instead of correcting their views accordingly, they were not helped by it.

> Human reason, therefore, neither approaches, nor strives toward, nor even takes a straight aim at, this truth: to understand who the true God is or what sort of God he wishes to be toward us.[50]

Even though pagan authors may have some accidental insight, they respond wrongly to what knowledge they have. The philosophers, then, for all their intelligence, were no closer to God than the rest of humanity. They suppressed what truth they had and responded to it wrongly.

Calvin recognised that this viewpoint was difficult to accept; that, in itself, is a spiritual problem. We are 'drunk with the false opinion of our own insight'; it is human nature to pride ourselves on our cleverness. For that reason, we are 'extremely reluctant to admit that

---

[46] Calvin, *Institutes* II.ii.16 (Battles 1:275).
[47] Calvin, *Institutes* II.ii.17 (Battles 1:276).
[48] Calvin, *Institutes* II.ii.18 (Battles 1:277).
[49] Calvin, *Institutes* II.ii.18 (Battles 1:277).
[50] Calvin, *Institutes* II.ii.18 (Battles 1:278).

it is utterly blind and stupid in divine matters'.[51] So we need Scripture to teach us even this basic truth. Actual knowledge of God, as opposed to occasional flashes of truth that are misunderstood, or innate insight that is wrongly responded to, only comes from God through his Spirit. We need Scripture, and we need the Spirit to open our eyes to that Scripture. Even with the teaching of Scripture, we are only able to understand God's mysteries when 'illumined by God's grace'.[52]

Just as sin has a noetic affect, then, so does grace. The faith that is itself a gift of God trusts and believes God, and so believes his word.[53] This faith gives us *certainty* in our knowledge:

> Now we shall possess a right definition of faith if we call it a firm and certain knowledge of God's benevolence toward us, founded upon the truth of the freely given promise in Christ, both revealed to our minds and sealed upon our hearts through the Holy Spirit.[54]

The Spirit is our 'inner teacher', enabling us to believe and so know the truth of God's promises and have heavenly wisdom.[55] It gives us knowledge that God is our Father and 'that Christ has been given to us as righteousness, sanctification, and life'.[56] It enables us to have the knowledge of God through Scripture, to know him not just as creator but in Christ as Redeemer.[57] It gives us the spiritual insight to know God, know his fatherly care, and know how to live according to his law.[58]

Calvin, then, has the same trajectory as Augustine: faith seeking understanding. Faith is the prerequisite of true understanding, true

---

[51] Calvin, *Institutes* II.ii.19 (Battles 1:278).
[52] Calvin, *Institutes* II.ii.21 (Battles 1:281).
[53] Calvin, *Institutes* III.ii.7 (Battles 1:550).
[54] Calvin, *Institutes* III.ii.7 (Battles 1:551).
[55] Calvin, *Institutes* III.i.4 (Battles 1:541-2).
[56] Calvin, *Institutes* III.ii.2 (Battles 1:545).
[57] Calvin, *Institutes* I.vi.1 (Battles 1:70-71).
[58] Calvin, *Institutes* II.ii.18 (Battles 1:277).

knowledge of God. It is a little frustrating that Calvin did not work through the consequences of this more fully. He does not go into detail, for instance, as to how faith restores natural reason. Calvin clearly expects people to use their reason and understanding in hearing the word, learning it, and learning good theology from it (the existence of the *Institutes* at all is testimony to this). However, for all he is a great theologian, Calvin is not much of a philosopher. He presents no general reflections on how our minds, and our use of reason, are affected by the illumination of grace after salvation.

Perhaps this is because Calvin, like Luther, also has a great suspicion of a kind of speculative theology. '[It] is not for us to attempt with bold curiosity to penetrate to the investigation of his essence, which we ought more to adore than meticulously to search out'.[59] Our knowledge is meant to teach us 'fear and reverence', to seek good from God and thank him for it.[60] The rule of 'modesty and sobriety' to which we ought to hold in doctrine is 'not to speak, or guess, or even seek to know, concerning obscure matters except what has been imparted to us by God's Word'.[61]

---

[59] Calvin, *Institutes* I.v.9 (Battles 1:62).
[60] Calvin, *Institutes* I.ii.2 (Battles 1:41-42).
[61] Calvin, *Institutes* I.xiv.4 (Battles 1:164).

4. Conclusion

We twenty-first century thinkers live in an empiricist and post-Enlightenment world, where our own ability to construct knowledge from what our senses tell us is considered the high watermark of human achievement. We have unbounded faith in our ability to know because of our own powers of observation and deduction. At the same time, we have completely undermined our ability to know in the postmodern questioning of knowledge claims, in the acknowledgement of our inescapable boundedness to a subjective point of view and the human tendency for knowledge claims to degenerate to power claims.

The Reformation acknowledged both. We are inescapably limited. We are hopelessly fallen. Where does our confidence in knowledge therefore lie? In God, who is neither. God speaks, and so we can know. God enables us to listen to his infallible word. Faith, itself a gift from God, is the way to certain knowledge. In the face of uncertainty about knowledge claims which has been with us since the ancients, the Word of God provides salvation.

4.1. Further reading:

Anderson, David, 2012. *Martin Luther: the problem of faith and reason; a re-examination in light of the epistemological and Christological issues* (Eugene, Oregon: Wipf and Stock).

Gerrish, B. A., 1962. *Grace and Reason: A Study in the Theology of Luther* (Oxford: Oxford University Press).

W. Andrew Hoffecker (ed), 1986. *Building a Christian World View Vol I God, Man and Knowledge* (Phillipsburg, NJ: Presbyterian and Reformed Publishing Company).

Dewey J. Hoitenga, Jr, 1991. *Faith and Reason from Plato to Plantinga: An Introduction to Reformed Epistemology* (Albany: State University of New York Press).

Nagel, Jennifer, 2014. *Knowledge: A Very Short Introduction* (Oxford: Oxford University Press).

Parker, T. H. L, 1969. *The Doctrine of the Knowledge of God: a Study in the Theology of John Calvin* (Edinburgh: Oliver and Boyd).

St. Antholin's Lectureship Charity Lectures

In or about 1559 the parish of St. Antholin, now absorbed into what is the parish of St Mary-le-Bow in Cheapside and St Mary Aldermanbury, within the Cordwainer's Ward in the City of London, came into the possession of certain estates known as the 'Lecturer's Estates.' These were, it is believed, purchased with funds collected at or shortly after the date of the Reformation for the endowment of lectures, mid-week sermons or talks by Puritan preachers.

Over the centuries the funds were not always used for the stated purpose, and in the first part of the nineteenth century a scheme was drawn up which revivified the lectureship, which was to consist of forty lectures to be given three times a year on the "Puritan School of Divinity", the lecturer to receive one guinea per lecture. A further onerous requirement was that the lecturer had to be a beneficed Anglican, living within one mile of the Mansion House in the City of London.

Under such conditions the lectureship fell into disuse a long time ago, and it was not until 1987 that moves were put in hand with the Charity Commissioners to update the scheme. The first lecture under the new scheme was given in 1991.

Trustees: The Reverend W.T. Taylor

The Reverend Dr. M.E. Burkill

The Reverend Dr. L. Gatiss

1991	J.I. Packer, *A Man for All Ministries: Richard Baxter 1651-1691*.
1992	Geoffrey Cox, *The Recovery and Renewal of the Local Church: the Puritan Vision*.
1993	Alister E. McGrath, *Evangelical Spirituality – Past Glories – Present Hopes – Future Possibilities*.
1994	Gavin J. McGrath, *'But We Preach Christ Crucified': The Cross of Christ in the Pastoral Theology of John Owen*.
1995	Peter Jensen, *Using the Shield of Faith – Puritan Attitudes to Combat with Satan*.
1996	J.I. Packer, *An Anglican to Remember – William Perkins: Puritan Popularizer*.
1997	Bruce Winter, *Pilgrim's Progress and Contemporary Evangelical Piety*.
1998	Peter Adam, *A Church 'Halfly Reformed' – the Puritan Dilemma*.
1999	J.I. Packer, *The Pilgrim's Principles: John Bunyan Revisited*.
2000	Ashley Null, *Conversion to Communion: Thomas Cranmer on a Favourite Puritan Theme*.
2001	Peter Adam, *Word and Spirit: The Puritan-Quaker Debate*.
2002	Wallace Benn, *Usher on Bishops: A Reforming Ecclesiology*.
2003	Peter Ackroyd, *Strangers to Correction: Christian Discipline and the English Reformation*.
2004	David Field, *'Decalogue' Dod and his Seventeenth Century Bestseller: A Four Hundredth Anniversary Appreciation*.
2005	Chad B. Van Dixhoorn, *A Puritan Theology of Preaching*.
2006	Peter Adam, *'To Bring Men to Heaven by Preaching' – John Donne's Evangelistic Sermons*.
2007	Tony Baker, *1807 – 2007: John Newton and the Twenty-first Century*.
2008	Lee Gatiss, *From Life's First Cry: John Owen on Infant Baptism and Infant Salvation*.
2009	Andrew Atherstone, *Evangelical Mission and Anglican Church Order: Charles Simeon Reconsidered*
2010	David Holloway, *Re-establishing the Christian Faith – and the Public Theology Deficit*.
2011	Andrew Cinnamond, *What matters in reforming the Church? Puritan Grievances under Elizabeth I*.
2012	Peter Adam, *Gospel Trials in 1662: To stay or to go?*
2013	Lee Gatiss, *Edmund Grindal – The Preacher's Archbishop*
2014	Lee Gatiss, *"Strangely Warmed" – Whitefield, Toplady, Simeon and Wesley's Arminian Campaigns*

St Antholin's Lectureship Charity Lectures

2015   Richard Turnbull, *Transformed Heart, Transforming Church: The Countess of Huntingdon's Connexion*

2016   Martyn Cowan, *Lessons from the Preaching of John Owen (1616–1683)*

2017   Kirsten Birkett, *And The Light Shineth In Darkness: Faith, Reason and Knowledge in the Reformation*

ed. Lee Gatiss, *Pilgrims, Warriors, and Servants: Puritan Wisdom for Today's Church: St Antholin lectures 1991-2000*

ed. Lee Gatiss, *Preachers, Pastors, and Ambassadors: Puritan Wisdom for Today's Church: St Antholin Lectures 2001-2010*